IDENTIFY THE IMBALANCE OF CONTROL DRAMAS

REFRAIN FROM GIVING A "PIECE OF YOUR MIND" AND FIND YOUR "PEACE OF MIND"

by Dr. Jody Janati

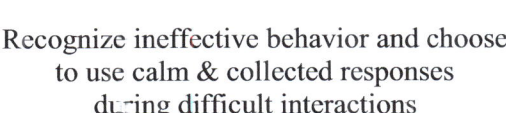

Recognize ineffective behavior and choose
to use calm & collected responses
during difficult interactions

Identify the Imbalance of Control Dramas: Refrain from Giving a "Piece of Your Mind" & Find Your "Peace of Mind"

Copyright © 2012 by Dr. Jody Janati
All rights reserved. No part of this book may be reproduced without written permission from the author.

Cover Photo: Someone's hands want to destruct equilibrium
Copyright © Dmitriy Kalinin - Fotolia.com

May You Find Your "Conversation Peace"

Table of Contents

Introduction 6

Chapter 1 7
Identify a Control Drama

Chapter 2 10
Identify Intimidator Behavior

Chapter 3 33
Identify Poor Me Behavior

Chapter 4 55
Identify Interrogator Behavior

Chapter 5 78
Identify Aloof Behavior

Chapter 6 102
Identify Strategies to Best Balance a Control Drama

Introduction

Most people have come to accept that conflict is inevitable, but what they may not realize is most of us use control dramas to essentially "get our way with others" to gain attention and power. We get our way with others by making them pay attention to us and then elicit a certain reaction from them to make ourselves feel fulfilled. The positive feelings we gain are won at the expense of the other person and this often causes imbalance and drama in our interpersonal relationships.

Your feelings can essentially tell you how you are doing at any given point in time. You will be able to identify and work through the personal emotions that arise in the presence of a control drama. The insights gained from exploration of your feelings, will allow you to constructively manage your emotions and ultimately engage others more authentically. In this book you'll learn about common control dramas and how to negate them through step by step applied approaches that really work.

CHAPTER 1
IDENTIFY A CONTROL DRAMA

A control drama, as coined by James Redfield in his book, "The Celestine Prophecy," is played by anyone who is feeling low on power or energy, to manipulate and steal the energy of another. Control dramas are unconscious strategies all people use to gain power or energy from another person and to essentially, "get their way with others." We get our way with others by making them pay attention to us and then elicit a certain reaction from them to make ourselves feel fulfilled. The positive feelings we gain are won at the expense of the other person and this often causes imbalance and drama in our interpersonal relationships.

Most of us have a dominant control drama in which we engage in automatically, without even realizing what we are doing and to what extent and expense. Your need to defend and engage in defensive responses with someone means you are caught in a control drama and you will thus, "react." When you start to become aware of your dominant control drama and can recognize it in action, you can start to hone it and make better choices in your responses to others. Likewise, once you understand how others use control dramas to make you react, you can refrain from engaging in them and move on to more healthy resolution "responses."

As you learn more about control dramas, you will realize you are already quite familiar with them and this is because you have been exposed to a variety of people throughout your life and have had to test each of them to successfully navigate intense interactions. Most people will resort to the same control drama when feeling tested and are completely unaware of it and how others experience them during these episodes. And with awareness, comes change.

Awareness and recognition of a control drama allows you to break the cycle and choose to disconnect from it altogether. When a control drama isn't controlling an interaction, you can "respond" more effectively and authentically to others. You will learn about four common control dramas people use to attract and defeat others. You will also discover there are many effective ways to approach others during difficult interactions. Knowing you have choices during difficult interactions with others, allows you to live a drama free life and helps you find your "conversation peace."

CHAPTER 2
IDENTIFY INTIMIDATOR BEHAVIOR

Recognizable Behavior of an Intimidator Response

- Quick to argue or yell

- May pick a fight or bad mouth you

- Communication has an arrogant tone

- Attempts to control things/others

- Prone to unexpected outbursts

- Self-obsessed – it feels like they want "center stage"

- Often stand too close – it feels like they corner you

- Lack of empathy – emotionally limited

Common Communication Patterns of Intimidator Behavior

- "Do this for me"
- "I guarantee you that…"
- "Here's what really happened"
- "I am just telling the truth/being honest"
- "Me first"
- Statements are often framed in the negative
- An intimidator sticks to conversations concerning the facts

Power Moves used by Intimidator Behavior to Elicit Attention from Others

- Breaks the other's spirit - "why would anyone want that job?"
- Steals their "thunder" - interrupts with "let me tell you what really happened…"

- Creates a threatening atmosphere

Point of View/Potential Underlying Fear of Intimidator Behavior

You may be wondering why some people engage in intimidator behavior. Behavior is perpetuated by fear. For example, if you are afraid of a snake, you might jump up and run away when you come across one. Some common fears of people who engage in intimidator behavior are that they can't be wrong or are not allowed the luxury of not knowing the answer.

These fears are intense and very real to the individual who holds them. They may have an underlying belief that mirrors, "it is better to do it to them, then to have it done to me." They feel the need to stand out and be noticed and when this doesn't happen they use intimidator behavior to ensure it will.

Common Destructive Communication Strategies of Intimidator Behavior

- Criticizing - "you always/you never…" "you are the most stubborn…"

- Judging - "that's the craziest idea…" "I guarantee you that this will not work…"

Intimidators Often Use a Competing Conflict Response Style

During an intense interaction, the interpersonal style of conflict you will typically find coupled with intimidator behavior is competition. Competitive messages include feelings of "Might makes right" and like a shark, competitors are willing to use force when needed.

Common competitive behavior includes the willingness to take quick action and many people who are comfortable using competitive responses will find themselves in situations where they have to make unpopular decisions for a group. They often focus on and manage vital issues within a group of people [family or workplace]. They may need to act as the protection and because of this, they are comfortable with attempting direct confrontation with others and are willing to push others to change.

Competitors are skilled at many things. They have the ability to argue or debate to make a legitimate point. They can use rank or influence when needed and will share their opinions openly so you know where they stand. If someone challenges their stance, they have the ability to state their position clearly and stand their ground.

There are a number of positive and negative consequences that result from competitive behavior. If competition is overused it will result in a lack of feedback from others in the group. Reduced learning and know how will occur when the competitive person takes the reins and does most of the work. This may lead to a group feeling of low empowerment and the competitive person will find they are surrounded by "yes people" who give all of their power to them.

If competitive behavior is underused, you can expect restricted influence over a group as they won't know what to do when the behavior is gone. When a competitive person holds back too much, indecision by others occurs as they are left waiting for a reaction. This delay from the competitor causes others to be slow to act and they will likely withhold their contributions within the group.

Most people who predominantly exhibit intimidator behavior initially approach conflict with a response that suggests, "It is my way or the highway." However, when engaged in an intense interpersonal drama, which ends with the intimidator feeling defeated, you can expect them to exhibit behavioral responses in this order during the escalation: intimidator, interrogator, poor me and then they will end with aloof behavior.

What You'll Experience in the Presence of Intimidator Behavior

- Discomfort in their presence [uneasy]

- Their "truth" is often felt as an insult

- A message of entitlement

- A feeling of being drained

- Exhaustion or lack of energy

- An unsafe or threatening tone

- The lack of control

Why Am I Uneasy in the Presence of Intimidator Behavior?

Intimidator behavior will evoke particular feelings for the receiver as these responses control us around our common human need to be safe. In other words, intimidator responses play off of our self-doubt and fear and this is how we both plug into and are controlled by them. The underlying feeling of an intimidator response is, "I have all the power and you will answer to me." To maintain inner balance in the presence of intimidator behavior we need to overcome our negative personal emotions related to these fears or we may give our power and energy to them and/or lose our acceptance and love for them. Below are some examples of common thoughts and feelings that arise in the presence of intimidator behavior:

- "I am in danger, I could be hurt."

- "I am being threatened."

- "I feel a sense of injustice around this person; s/he is not being fair."

- "I feel like something horrible could happen."

- "I have no control right now."

- "I must be wrong because this person is shouting at me."

- "I am unable to protect myself from this person."

- "I am weak and cannot protect my needs and beliefs."

- "I think it might be better to give in and have peace than stand up for what I need or believe."

- "I have no power in this situation."

- "I cannot be myself in the presence of this person."

- "I am exhausted when interacting with this person."

- "I am unable to function out of the fear I feel in this person's presence."

- "I am unworthy and feel rejected by this person."

- "I have a sense of guilt about my choices when interacting with this person."

- "I am hurt this person doesn't understand me and my choices."

- "I feel bitter; this person thinks s/he can shame me about my life and my choices."

- "I am completely humiliated and demeaned by this person."

- "I am angry s/he thinks s/he can treat me this way."

- "I am drained of energy around this person and cannot offer anything in return to her/him."

- "I am frustrated and angry with her/him because s/he is preventing me from feeling good."

Intimidator Behavior Elicits Negative Counter Behavior from Others

- Intimidators will experience the lack of feedback and indecision from others

- Intimidators will have reduced learning, as others withhold information from them

- Intimidators usually take the lead/do and the result is low empowerment of others

- Intimidators find themselves surrounded by "yes people" who are slow to act

What Personal Benefits are Gained at the Expense of Using Intimidator Behavior?

When someone engages in intimidator behavior they will experience a number of personal benefits. Intimidator behavior allows one to control others and essentially get their way with others by making people fear them. The use of intimidator behavior allows people to feel a false sense of security because when they are engaged in it:

- They don't have to look at themselves or work on their own issues because everyone else is wrong and only the others need to change.

- They create fear in others and thus are able to gain power and attention [a personal need].

- They get to be in a position where no one will approach them or "burden" them for anything.

- They get to be right at the expense of others being wrong and get to police them.

- They get to decide for everyone and therefore get their way.

Common Clashes to Intimidator Behavior

Intimidators tend to feel the most uncomfortable, misunderstood and defensive around people who tend to use aloof behavior. There is an old adage that states, "what you don't like about others is usually something you don't like about yourself" and this saying starts to resonate upon further investigation as to why individuals with intimidator and aloof behavior do not intermingle well after long periods of time.

It has been previously noted that when intimidators are at their worst [defeated], they will go through the drama cycle and are forced to give in when they reach aloof behavior. When intimidators spend time with people who use aloof behavior, they are reminded of what they feel like and how they respond to others when they are at their worst and feeling weak. This can become downright repulsive when the aloof behavior is recognized and fixated upon.

Common Alliances to Intimidator Behavior

Intimidators will often most strongly align with and defend family members and friends who tend to use intimidator and interrogator behavior. Simply put, intimidators understand, condone and can justify the behavior of other intimidators and because of this, they often get along well. Intimidators can abruptly extinguish interrogator behavior with statements like, "well, if you died, the whole world would fall apart;" while, likewise, interrogators can abruptly extinguish intimidator behavior with statements like, "yes, drill sergeant; who died and made you the boss?"

When a control drama is called out and brought to the forefront, it cannot stay active for much longer and thus intimidator and interrogator behavior often cancel one another out. The result is that the two individuals will spend longer periods of time together. There also seems to be an unconscious understanding that if these two behavior types were to have a conflict, it could be intense because the intimidator is never wrong and the interrogator can ask a million and one questions. The risk is that the conflict might never end.

You will find that when two individuals have the same dominant control drama, yet they do not get along, it is usually based on one's rationale of the other's intention behind the behavior they are displaying. [i.e. It is said that "if you can spot it, you got it," meaning, the individual will clearly recognize the behavior, but doesn't agree with the other's use of it or the intended purpose behind it].

Common Long Term Attraction to Intimidator Behavior

Intimidators tend to be most strongly drawn to and attracted to people who tend to use poor me behavior. Those who use intimidator behaviors do not feel "right" in the presence of guilt, so poor me behaviors easily throw them off balance and gain their attention. Poor me behavior will accommodate the demands of intimidator behavior and can easily create guilt to attach to it.

Effective Approaches that Help Distance You from Intimidator Behavior

- Avoid putting yourself in a position where you must rely on an intimidator [advice, a loan, carpooling]

- Ask directly about their need to repeat their point after you've expressed yours

- Avoid the compulsion to defend yourself by meeting their behavior with silence

- Choose to frame conversation topics to their benefit

- Limit your disclosure of emotion and personal experiences

- Make certain topics off limits

Maintain Inner Balance When Dealing with Intimidator Behavior

When dealing with intimidator responses, we need to deal with some personal emotions in order to stay steady in their presence and not be affected by them. You can use positive affirmations, like the examples below, to maintain balance when dealing with intimidator behavior:

- "I am safe and secure in this situation."

- "This person is a teacher, who life has placed before me."

- "S/he is unhappy and afraid, or else s/he would not be acting this way."

- "Behind her/his angry and threatening appearance hides a fearful and hurt person."

- "Life gives me experiences I need so I can grow."

- "We all have different ways of viewing things."

- "I am not responsible for this person's choices."

- "People can get along and love each other even when they don't agree."

- "No one can use me so I will choose to give or not to give to this person."

- "I don't need to explain my decisions to this person."

- "This person is helping me better understand my own needs."

Understanding Intimidator Behavior Leads to Acceptance and Forgiveness

How do you feel when you believe someone is intentionally intimidating or controlling you? Choose one specific person to focus on and be precise about what you think of that individual. I suggest you write down your feelings to really grasp how you experience this person and feel in their presence. How might you view that person differently once you can fully grasp and trust that "they do not know what they do?"

Most intimidators have the intention of offering their truth or the facts to your life experience. Reexamine an intense interaction you've had with an intimidator and see if you can change your point of view to now hear their message with the intention of assisting you with facts. How do you feel about this person when you don't see them as intimidating? Is there any reason to keep labeling them this way? Move towards accepting the individual for who s/he is, knowing that "people don't change; responses change" and choose to change your responses when in the presence of intimidator behavior. You are in control of your experiences with others and can choose whether or not you will engage their control drama.

Exercise 1: Work Through Your Personal Emotions Related to Intimidator Behavior

Start by imagining someone who creates defensiveness within you through their intimidating behavior. The following are words we use when we want to express a combination of emotional states and physical sensations. This list, compiled by the center for nonviolent communication, is neither exhaustive nor definitive. It is meant as a starting place to support anyone who wishes to engage in a process of deepening self-discovery and to facilitate greater understanding and connection between people. Circle the negative feelings that arise in you when you are interacting with this person:

- afraid • apprehensive • dread • foreboding • frightened • mistrustful • panicked • petrified • scared • suspicious • terrified • wary • worried • annoyed • aggravated • dismayed • disgruntled • displeased • exasperated • frustrated • impatient • irritated • irked • angry • enraged • furious • incensed • indignant • irate • livid • outraged • resentful • aversion • animosity • appalled • contempt • disgusted • dislike • hate • horrified • hostile • repulsed • confused • ambivalent • baffled • bewildered • dazed • hesitant • lost • mystified • perplexed • puzzled • torn • disconnected • alienated • aloof • apathetic • bored • cold • detached • distant • distracted • indifferent • numb • removed • uninterested • withdrawn • disquiet • agitated • alarmed • discombobulated • disconcerted • disturbed • perturbed • rattled • restless • shocked • started • surprised • troubled • turbulent • turmoil

• uncomfortable • uneasy • unnerved • unsettled • upset • embarrassed • ashamed • chagrined flustered • guilty • mortified • self-conscious • fatigued • beat • burnt out • depleted exhausted • lethargic • listless • sleepy • tired • weary • worn out • pain • agony • anguished • bereaved • tense • anxious • cranky • distressed • distraught • edgy • fidgety • frazzled • irritable • jittery • nervous • overwhelmed • restless • stressed out • vulnerable • fragile • guarded • helpless • insecure • leery • reserved

(c) 2005 by Center for Nonviolent Communication
Website: www.cnvc.org Email: cnvc@cnvc.org
Phone: +1.505-244-4041

Exercise 2: Discover Your Voice

Write some advice you would like to give to this person when you are feeling defensive. Use the following words to create up to 5 suggestive statements for this person [Should, Need to, Shouldn't, and Ought to]. For example, you might write, "S/he ought to keep her opinions to herself," or "S/he shouldn't tell me what to do with my life," or "S/he needs to get a job."

1

2

3

4

5

Exercise 3: Explore Your Unmet Needs

Review your advice from the list above and contemplate what need is not being met by exploring the implication of each of your original statements. For example, when reflecting on the statement, "s/he shouldn't tell me what to do with my life," you may find that you are upset because you need acceptance and support for your well-being. The statement, "S/he needs to get a job," might be pointing to your own need for security and your fear for their well-being.

The following list of needs, compiled by the center for nonviolent communication, is neither exhaustive nor definitive. It is meant as a starting place to support anyone who wishes to engage in a process of deepening self-discovery and to facilitate greater understanding and connection between people. Reread your suggestive statements from exercise two and circle the positive feelings, below, you would rather experience when interacting with this person.

● affection ● appreciation ● belonging ● cooperation ● communication ● closeness ● community ● companionship ● compassion ● consideration ● consistency ● empathy ● inclusion ● intimacy ● love ● mutuality ● nurturing ● respect/self-respect ● safety ● security ● stability ● support ● to know and be known ● to see and be seen ● to understand and be understood ● trust ● warmth ● physical well-being ● air ● food ● movement/exercise ● rest/sleep ● sexual expression ● safety ● shelter ● touch ● water ● honesty ● authenticity ● integrity ● presence ● play ● joy ● humor ● peace ● beauty ● communion ● ease ● equality ● harmony ● inspiration ● order ● autonomy ● choice ● freedom ● independence ● space ● spontaneity ● meaning ● awareness ● celebration of life ● challenge ● clarity ● competence ● consciousness ● contribution ● creativity ● discovery ● efficacy ● effectiveness ● growth ● hope ● learning

• mourning • participation • purpose • self-expression • stimulation • to matter • understanding

(c) 2005 by Center for Nonviolent Communication
Website: www.cnvc.org Email: cnvc@cnvc.org
Phone: +1.505-244-4041

CHAPTER 3
IDENTIFY POOR ME BEHAVIOR

Recognizable Behavior of a Poor Me Response

- Looks worried and sighs often

- Speaks slower than you when you speak

- Mentions their unfortunate experiences

- When help is offered they reject it

- Discusses the same topic with you often

- Shows little responsibility for actions

Common Communication Pattern of Poor Me Behavior

- Retells the same drawn out stories

- A poor me sticks to conversations concerning cliché statements [what a nice day; this is some weather we're having hey?]

- "Yeah, but…" – agrees then denies

Power Moves used to Elicit Attention from Others

- Gets attention by eliciting pity or guilt

- Thrives in drama or when rehashing a problem [even subtle dramas]

- May intentionally procrastinate, forget, sulk or communicate a personal inefficiency

- Creates a sense of obligation for you

Point of View/Potential Underlying Fear

You may be wondering why some people engage in poor me behavior. Behavior is perpetuated by fear. For example, if you are afraid of a snake, you might jump up and run away when you come across one. Some common fears of people who engage in poor me behavior are that they can't rely on others to meet their personal needs and they aren't supposed to ask for or pursue their needs directly.

These fears are intense and very real to the individual who holds them. They feel the need to be noticed and validated as equal and when this doesn't happen they use poor me behavior to ensure it will.

Common Destructive Communication Strategies of Poor Me Behavior

> ▪Defensiveness [used to protect themselves against pain, fear, etc.]
>
> ▪Whining, deflecting, denying or further defending
>
> ▪Minimizing - "you'll make it work…" "Don't worry, I am fine, this will pass."

A Poor Me Often Uses an Accommodating Conflict Response Style

During an intense interaction, the interpersonal style of conflict you will typically find coupled with poor me behavior is accommodation. Accommodating messages include feelings of "I'll kill them with kindness" and like a teddy bear, accommodators are willing to sooth and smooth things out.

Common accommodating behavior includes the ability to yield and this will usually be done with either gladness or bitterness. Accommodators can show reasonableness when working with a group and because of this, they are able to develop performance in those around them. They understand how to create good will and keep the peace. They often focus on and manage issues of low importance within a group of people [family or workplace].

Accommodators are skilled at many things. They have the ability to forgo their own desires for the needs of others and because of this, you will often feel a real selflessness about them. They will usually obey orders when working with others and have the ability to yield to new ideas.

There are a number of positive and negative consequences that result from accommodating behavior. If accommodation is overused it will result in others ignoring them and their ideas will get little attention. The more they accommodate others, the more restricted their influence becomes when working with a group. As a result, accommodators may experience a loss of contribution from others or complete anarchy.

If accommodating behavior is underused, you can expect a change in the morale from others where they will start to lack rapport with the accommodator. If an accommodator changes his/her response too dramatically, others will feel they are no longer willing to bend and suddenly exceptions will no longer be recognized in others; this will likely upset the people in the group.

Most people who predominantly exhibit poor me behavior initially approach conflict with a response that suggests, "It would be my pleasure to accommodate you." However, when engaged in an intense interpersonal drama, which ends with the poor me feeling defeated, you can expect them to exhibit behavioral responses in this order during the escalation: poor me, aloof, intimidator and then they will end with interrogator behavior.

What You'll Experience in the Presence of Poor Me Behavior

- A sense of guilt

- An obligation to help

- A responsibility to accommodate their needs

- Pity for them

- A feeling that they need you

Why Am I Uneasy in the Presence of Poor Me Behavior?

Poor me behavior will evoke particular feelings for the receiver as these responses control us around our common human need to be worthy through helping others and being of assistance. In other words, poor me responses play off of our need for approval, self-recognition and self-worth and this is how we both plug into and are controlled by them. The underlying feeling of a poor me response is "you are not doing enough for me right now."

To maintain inner balance in the presence of poor me behavior we need to overcome our negative personal emotions related to these fears or we may give our power and energy to them and/or lose our acceptance and love for them. Below are some examples of common thoughts and feelings that arise in the presence of poor me behavior:

- "I feel angry because this person is not doing what s/he should be doing for him/herself."

- "I am responsible for his/her reality."

- "I am worthy only if s/he is satisfied with me and with what I offer her/him."

- "I am to blame when s/he isn't feeling happy or satisfied."

- "I need approval and recognition for what I have done and am doing for with this person."

- "I feel helpless in the presence of this person."

- "I feel a sense of injustice because I helped her/him and s/he is not satisfied."

- "I need to be of better assistance to her/him."

- "I am nervous I won't succeed in helping this person."

- "I am bitter because of her/his failure to recognize my efforts."

- "I feel guilty because s/he isn't satisfied with me."

- "I am angry at her/him because s/he is not doing what s/he should be doing."

- "I think others are weak and need my help; I must save others."

- "I am afraid for her/his well-being; I am stronger, know better and can help them."

- "The more people I save, the worthier I am."

- "I am afraid I am not able to succeed in helping her/him and I will be responsible."

- "I feel hurt and rejected because s/he never recognizes my efforts or my love."

- "It is my fault s/he hurts and I feel frustrated because I am not allowed to help her/him."

- "I feel angry because s/he is controlling me; I am now the victim's victim."

- "I am angry s/he thinks s/he can treat me this way."

- "I am drained of energy around this person and cannot offer anything in return to her/him."

- "I am frustrated and angry with her/him because s/he is preventing me from feeling good."

Poor Me Behavior Elicits Negative Counter Behavior from Others

- Others will choose to have a surface level relationship with you

- People will give the poor me's ideas very little attention once expressed

- Poor me's will not be included in the decision making process

- People experience poor me behavior as sneaky and/or snide

What Personal Benefits are Gained at the Expense of Using Poor Me Behavior?

When someone engages in poor me behavior they will experience a number of personal benefits. Poor me behavior allows one to control others and essentially get their way with others by making people feel obligated to help/listen to them, etc. The use of poor me behavior allows people to feel a false sense of security because when they are engaged in it:

- They don't have to be responsible for what's happening to them.

- They can control others with guilt, pity and obligation to gain power and attention [fulfill a personal need].

- They feel automatic self-esteem/self-worth as people give attention to them and their issues.

- They get others to do things for them and therefore they don't have to carry the burden.

Common Clashes to Poor Me Behavior

A poor me tends to feel the most uncomfortable, misunderstood and defensive around people who tend to use interrogator behavior. There is an old adage that states, "what you don't like about others is usually something you don't like about yourself" and this saying starts to resonate upon further investigation as to why individuals with poor me and interrogator behavior do not intermingle well after long periods of time.

It has been previously noted that when a poor me is at his/her worst [defeated], s/he will go through the drama cycle and are forced to give in when they reach interrogator behavior. When a poor me spends time with people who use interrogator behavior, they are reminded of what they feel like and how they respond to others when they are at their worst and feeling weak. This can become downright repulsive when the interrogator behavior is recognized and fixated upon.

Common Alliances to Poor Me Behavior

A poor me will often most strongly align with and defend family members and friends who tend to use poor me and aloof behavior. Simply put, a poor me understands, condones and can justify the behavior of another poor me and because of this, they often get along well. A poor me can abruptly extinguish aloof behavior with statements like, "what's wrong; I feel bad when you don't talk to me; did I do something to make you upset" while, likewise, an aloof can abruptly extinguish poor me behavior with statements like, "uh huh, what," while they appear to not hear what the poor me is in the midst of saying.

When a control drama is called out and brought to the forefront, it cannot stay active for much longer and thus poor me and aloof behavior often cancel one another out. The result is that the two individuals will spend longer periods of time together. There also seems to be an unconscious understanding that if these two behavior types were to have a conflict, it could be intense because the poor me can hold a grudge/guilt for long periods of time and the aloof can withdraw and play the silent treatment for long periods of time. The risk is that the conflict might never end.

You will find that when two individuals have the same dominant control drama, yet they do not get along, it is usually based on one's rationale of the other's intention behind the behavior they are displaying. [i.e. It is said that "if you can spot it, you got it," meaning, the individual will clearly recognize the behavior, but doesn't agree with the other's use of it or the intended purpose behind it].

Common Long Term Attraction to Poor Me Behavior

A poor me tends to be most strongly drawn to and attracted to people who tend to use intimidator behavior. Those who use poor me behavior can find pity from the demands of an intimidator and intimidators cannot be "right" in the presence of guilt and thus, the poor me can capture their attention.

Effective Approaches that Help Distance You from Poor Me Behavior

- Ask directly about their reluctance to let you help them

- Directly tell them that you are more interested in solving their problems then continuing to rehash them

- Assure them you have chosen to hold positive thoughts for them as they work through their issue and then change the subject

Maintain Inner Balance When Dealing with Poor Me Behavior

When dealing with poor me responses, we need to deal with some personal emotions in order to stay steady in their presence and not be affected by them. You can use positive affirmations, like the examples below, to maintain balance when dealing with poor me behavior:

- "I am not to blame for what others are experiencing in their lives."

- "I can experience someone without being sad because they are not happy."

- "It is not my job to save this person."

- "Sometimes the greatest help is to let others find their own way and figure it out."

- "I cannot assist her/him with this problem now and that doesn't mean I am unlovable."

- "Life gives me experiences I need so I can grow."

- "We all have different ways of viewing things."

- "I am not responsible for this person's choices."

- "People can get along and love each other even when they don't agree."

- "No one can use me so I will choose to give or not to give to this person."

- "I don't need to explain my decisions to this person."

- "This person is helping me better understand my own needs."

Understanding Poor Me Behavior Leads to Acceptance and Forgiveness

How do you feel when you believe someone is intentionally making you feel guilty, obligated or sorry for them? Choose one specific person to focus on and be precise about what you think of that individual. I suggest you write down your feelings to really grasp how you experience this person and feel in their presence. How might you view that person differently once you can fully grasp and trust that "they do not know what they do?"

Most poor me behavior comes with the intention of being validated by you and your life experience. Reexamine an intense interaction you've had with poor me behavior and see if you can change your point of view to now hear their message with the intention of you seeing them as valid, equal and significant. How do you feel about this person when you don't see them as a poor me? Is there any reason to keep labeling them this way? Move towards accepting the individual for who s/he is, knowing that "people don't change; responses change" and choose to change your responses when in the presence of poor me behavior. You are in control of your experiences with others and can choose whether or not you will engage their control drama.

Exercise 1: Work Through Your Personal Emotions Related to Poor Me Behavior

Start by imagining someone who creates defensiveness within you through their poor me behavior. The following are words we use when we want to express a combination of emotional states and physical sensations. This list, compiled by the center for nonviolent communication, is neither exhaustive nor definitive. It is meant as a starting place to support anyone who wishes to engage in a process of deepening self-discovery and to facilitate greater understanding and connection between people. Circle the negative feelings that arise in you when you are interacting with this person:

- afraid • apprehensive • dread • foreboding •
frightened • mistrustful • panicked • petrified •
scared • suspicious • terrified • wary • worried •
annoyed • aggravated • dismayed • disgruntled •
displeased • exasperated • frustrated • impatient •
irritated • irked • angry • enraged • furious •
incensed • indignant • irate • livid • outraged •
resentful • aversion • animosity • appalled •
contempt • disgusted • dislike • hate • horrified •

hostile • repulsed • confused • ambivalent • baffled • bewildered • dazed • hesitant • lost • mystified • perplexed • puzzled • torn • disconnected • alienated • aloof • apathetic • bored • cold • detached • distant • distracted • indifferent • numb • removed • uninterested • withdrawn • disquiet • agitated • alarmed • discombobulated • disconcerted • disturbed • perturbed • rattled • restless • shocked • started • surprised • troubled • turbulent • turmoil • uncomfortable • uneasy • unnerved • unsettled • upset • embarrassed • ashamed • chagrined flustered • guilty • mortified • self-conscious • fatigued • beat • burnt out • depleted exhausted • lethargic • listless • sleepy • tired • weary • worn out • pain • agony • anguished • bereaved • tense • anxious • cranky • distressed • distraught • edgy • fidgety • frazzled • irritable • jittery • nervous • overwhelmed • restless • stressed out • vulnerable • fragile • guarded • helpless • insecure • leery • reserved

(c) 2005 by Center for Nonviolent Communication
Website: www.cnvc.org Email: cnvc@cnvc.org
Phone: +1.505-244-4041

Exercise 2: Discover Your Voice

Write some advice you would like to give to this person when you are feeling defensive. Use the following words to create up to 5 suggestive statements for this person [Should, Need to, Shouldn't, and Ought to]. For example, you might write, "S/he ought to keep her opinions to herself," or "S/he shouldn't tell me what to do with my life," or "S/he needs to get a job."

1

2

3

4

5

Exercise 3: Explore Your Unmet Needs

Review your advice from the list above and contemplate what need is not being met by exploring the implication of each of your original statements. For example, when reflecting on the statement, "s/he shouldn't tell me what to do with my life," you may find that you are upset because you need acceptance and support for your well-being. The statement, "S/he needs to get a job," might be pointing to your own need for security and your fear for their well-being.

The following list of needs, compiled by the center for nonviolent communication, is neither exhaustive nor definitive. It is meant as a starting place to support anyone who wishes to engage in a process of deepening self-discovery and to facilitate greater understanding and connection between people. Reread your suggestive statements from exercise two and circle the positive feelings, below, you would rather experience when interacting with this person.

- affection • appreciation • belonging • cooperation • communication • closeness • community • companionship • compassion • consideration • consistency • empathy • inclusion • intimacy • love • mutuality • nurturing • respect/self-respect • safety • security • stability • support • to know and be known • to see and be seen • to understand and be understood • trust • warmth • physical well-being • air • food • movement/exercise • rest/sleep • sexual expression • safety • shelter • touch • water • honesty • authenticity • integrity • presence • play • joy • humor • peace • beauty • communion • ease • equality • harmony • inspiration • order • autonomy • choice • freedom • independence • space • spontaneity • meaning • awareness • celebration of life • challenge • clarity • competence • consciousness • contribution • creativity • discovery • efficacy • effectiveness • growth • hope • learning • mourning • participation • purpose • self-expression • stimulation • to matter • understanding

(c) 2005 by Center for Nonviolent Communication
Website: www.cnvc.org Email: cnvc@cnvc.org
Phone: +1.505-244-4041

CHAPTER 4
IDENTIFY INTERROGATOR BEHAVIOR

Recognizable Behavior of an Interrogator Response

- Probes and instructs
- Must do it "their way"
- Suggests you aren't capable
- Sounds like a know-it-all
- Teaches and preaches
- Needles then offers self-righteous messages
- You "don't meet their standards"

Common Communication Pattern of Interrogator Behavior

- "Why?" followed by infallible logic
- "You should…I am just trying to help"

- "Did you ever consider…"

- "Here's what I did when that happened"

- An interrogator sticks to conversations concerning opinions

Power Moves used by Interrogator Behavior to Elicit Attention from Others

- Questions your every act or motive

- Dominates a conversation with questions

- Turns the topic of conversation back to them

- Scrutinizes your decisions/gives you pause

Point of View/Potential Underlying Fear of Interrogator Behavior

You may be wondering why some people engage in interrogator behavior. Behavior is perpetuated by fear. For example, if you are afraid of a snake, you might jump up and run away when you come across one. Some common fears of people who engage in interrogator behavior are that they will be betrayed or deserted and that they must be the hero and fix things for others.

These fears are intense and very real to the individual who holds them. They may have an underlying belief that mirrors, "if I want it done right then I will just have to do it myself" or "if I am not there, it will be done wrong." They feel the need to help others and tend to micromanage to hide their nervousness regarding things they can't let go or control and when this doesn't happen they use interrogator behavior to ensure it will.

Common Destructive Communication Strategies of Interrogator Behavior

> •Contempt - mockery, put-downs, hostile corrections, which may be coupled with sarcasm, ridicule, demeaning tone and outright joking. "How hard is it to xyz?"
>
> •Preaching - "Here's your problem and here's what I would do if I were you."

Interrogators Often Use a Compromising Conflict Response Style

During an intense interaction, the interpersonal style of conflict you will typically find coupled with interrogator behavior is compromise. Compromising messages include feelings of "Let's share" and like a fox, compromisers are willing to find a clever solution and split the difference.

Common compromising behavior includes the ability to demonstrate equal power with others. Compromisers maintain strong commitments and are capable of finding temporary solutions to problems that arise and because of this, they frequently play the role of "backup" for a group. They often focus on and manage issues of moderate importance within a group of people [family or workplace] and will find themselves dealing within many time constraints.

Compromisers are skilled at many things. They have the ability to negotiate well with others and will find a "middle ground." Their communication style is both assertive and cooperative and they focus on some gains and some losses for both sides involved. They are willing to make concessions and will give a little to get a little, which allows them the ability to assess the value of something.

There are a number of positive and negative consequences that result from compromising behavior. If compromise is overused it will result in the person losing the big picture or long term goals of a project. If someone compromises too much with others, they will experience a lack of trust from others and may find themselves in a more cynical climate.

If compromising behavior is underused, one can expect unnecessary confrontations from others who think they are now being treated unfairly. Once the ability to bend lessens, compromisers will find themselves in frequent power struggles with others and find they are now unable to negotiate effectively as they once did.

Most people who predominantly exhibit interrogator behavior initially approach conflict with a response that suggests, "Let's make a deal." However, when engaged in an intense interpersonal drama, which ends with the interrogator feeling defeated, you can expect them to exhibit behavioral responses in this order during the escalation: interrogator, intimidator, aloof and then they will end with poor me behavior.

What You'll Experience in the Presence of Interrogator Behavior

- A feeling of being monitored

- Your feelings are invalid

- Failure to meet their standards

- Being cast into the role of "inadequate"

- A message that "you can't handle it"

- A message regarding how you "should" feel

Why Am I Uneasy in the Presence of Interrogator Behavior?

Interrogator behavior will evoke particular feelings for the receiver as these responses control us around our common human need for approval and acceptance. In other words, interrogator responses play off of our need for recognition and self-esteem and this is how we both plug into and are controlled by them. The underlying feeling of an interrogator response is "I am questioning you and will make you doubt yourself and prove to me that you are right, capable, etc." To maintain inner balance in the presence of interrogator behavior we need to overcome our negative personal emotions related to these fears or we may give our power and energy to them and/or lose our acceptance and love for them. Below are some examples of common thoughts and feelings that arise in the presence of interrogator behavior:

> •"It is important I do not make mistakes and be right and I often fail at this."

> •"I feel guilty when I don't know how to be right in your presence."

> •"I feel angry because I want to be right too for my self-worth."

> •"I feel s/he wants me to act or feel differently than I do."

- "I feel a lot of self-doubt when s/he asks me questions."

- "I feel inadequate in the presence of this person."

- "I feel a lot of shame because I am not worthy unless s/he also agrees with me."

- "My self-worth is dependent on whether I make the right decisions and actions."

- "I feel s/he is watching me too closely and judging me."

- "I feel criticized by her/him because s/he does it better than I do."

- "I am not capable of doing it without her/his help."

- "I feel hurt that s/he lacks approval of my thoughts and actions."

- "I am not sure of myself in the presence of this person."

- "I might make a mistake and then s/he will reject me."

- "I need to prove to her/him that I am worthy and right."

- "I must have his/her approval to make my next choice."

- "I feel rejected and demeaned of my self-worth or intelligence around her/him."

- "I feel a sense of injustice because s/he is not being fair and is withholding her/his support."

- "I am being antagonized and need to prove that I am right and competent on this matter."

- "I am angry s/he thinks s/he can treat me this way."

- "I am drained of energy around this person and cannot offer anything in return to her/him."

- "I am frustrated and angry with her/him because s/he is preventing me from feeling good."

Interrogator Behavior Elicits Negative Counter Behavior from Others

- Interrogators often lose the big picture because they get caught up in details

- Interrogators experience a lack of trust from those around them

- Interrogators may find themselves in a cynical climate

What Personal Benefits are Gained at the Expense of Using Interrogator Behavior?

When someone engages in interrogator behavior they will experience a number of personal benefits. Interrogator behavior allows one to control others and essentially get their way with others by making others doubt themselves. The use of interrogator behavior allows people to feel a false sense of security because when they are engaged in it:

- They get to be right and more knowledgeable then everyone around them.

- They are able to make people doubt themselves and thus gain some personal power.

- They feel self-worth by focusing on others mistakes and faults and then get to avoid their own problems.

- They force others to need and rely upon their approval by questioning every move others make.

Common Clashes to Interrogator Behavior

Interrogators tend to feel the most uncomfortable, misunderstood and defensive around people who tend to use poor me behavior. There is an old adage that states, "what you don't like about others is usually something you don't like about yourself" and this saying starts to resonate upon further investigation as to why individuals with interrogator and poor me behavior do not intermingle well after long periods of time.

It has been previously noted that when interrogators are at their worst [defeated], they will go through the drama cycle and are forced to give in when they reach poor me behavior. When interrogators spend time with people who use poor me behavior, they are reminded of what they feel like and how they respond to others when they are at their worst and feeling weak. This can become downright repulsive when the poor me behavior is recognized and fixated upon.

Common Alliances to Interrogator Behavior

Interrogators will often most strongly align with and defend family members and friends who tend to use interrogator and intimidator behavior. Simply put, interrogators understand, condone and can justify the behavior of other interrogators and because of this, they often get along well. Interrogators can abruptly extinguish intimidator behavior with statements like, "who died and made you the boss?" while, likewise, intimidators can abruptly extinguish interrogator behavior with statements like, "well, if you died, the whole world would go unorganized."

When a control drama is called out and brought to the forefront, it cannot stay active for much longer and thus interrogator and intimidator behavior often cancel one another out. The result is that the two individuals will spend longer periods of time together. There also seems to be an unconscious understanding that if these two behavior types were to have a conflict, it could be intense because the interrogator can ask a million and one questions and the intimidator is never wrong. The risk is that the conflict might never end.

You will find that when two individuals have the same dominant control drama, yet they do not get along, it is usually based on one's rationale of the other's intention behind the behavior they are displaying. [i.e. It is said that "if you can spot it, you got it," meaning, the individual will clearly recognize the behavior, but doesn't agree with the other's use of it or the intended purpose behind it].

Common Long Term Attraction to Interrogator Behavior

Interrogators tend to be most strongly drawn to and attracted to people who tend to use aloof behavior. Those who use interrogator behavior like to ask questions and focus the conversation around their interests and the aloof is comfortable listening for longer periods of time because they get to avoid disclosure. Those who use aloof behaviors like to be drawn out and interrogators have the stamina to continue to ask the questions needed to get the aloof's attention.

Effective Approaches that Help Distance You From Interrogator Behavior

- Ask directly about their reason for questioning you

- Respond to their questions with questions [why do you ask, what do you mean]

- Make certain topics off limits

- Request they delegate tasks to you/others

Maintain Your Inner Balance When Dealing with Interrogator Behavior

When dealing with interrogator responses, we need to deal with some personal emotions in order to stay steady in their presence and not be affected by them. You can use positive affirmations, like the examples below, to maintain balance when dealing with interrogator behavior:

- "My self-worth is independent of what others think."

- "My self-worth is independent of the results of my efforts."

- "The interrogator is seeking self-esteem through my attention."

- "We can love each other even when we do not agree."

- "I am lovable even when II do not prove that I am right."

- "I am perfectly fine even when the other disagrees with me."

- "I learn through my mistakes."

- "I am not perfect and I make mistakes and I admit this without losing my self-worth or another's love."

- "Being right doesn't mean one is more acceptable than another."

- "Life gives me exactly what I need at that moment so that I can learn my next lesson in my personal growth."

- "Life gives me experiences I need so I can grow."

- "We all have different ways of viewing things."

- "I am not responsible for this person's choices."

- "People can get along and love each other even when they don't agree."

- "No one can use me so I will choose to give or not to give to this person."

- "I don't need to explain my decisions to this person."

- "This person is helping me better understand my own needs."

Understanding Interrogator Behavior Leads to Acceptance and Forgiveness

How do you feel when you believe someone is intentionally interrogating or monitoring you? Choose one specific person to focus on and be precise about what you think of that individual. I suggest you write down your feelings to really grasp how you experience this person and feel in their presence. How might you view that person differently once you can fully grasp and trust that "they do not know what they do?"

Most interrogators have the intention of helping you in your life experience. Reexamine an intense interaction you've had with an interrogator and see if you can change your point of view to now hear their message with the intention of assisting you with a project/decision/idea. How do you feel about this person when you don't see them as interrogating? Is there any reason to keep labeling them this way? Move towards accepting the individual for who s/he is, knowing that "people don't change; responses change" and choose to change your responses when in the presence of interrogator behavior. You are in control of your experiences with others and can choose whether or not you will engage their control drama.

Exercise 1: Work Through Your Personal Emotions Related to Interrogator Behavior

Start by imagining someone who creates defensiveness within you through their interrogating behavior. The following are words we use when we want to express a combination of emotional states and physical sensations. This list, compiled by the center for nonviolent communication, is neither exhaustive nor definitive. It is meant as a starting place to support anyone who wishes to engage in a process of deepening self-discovery and to facilitate greater understanding and connection between people. Circle the negative feelings that arise in you when you are interacting with this person:

● afraid ● apprehensive ● dread ● foreboding ● frightened ● mistrustful ● panicked ● petrified ● scared ● suspicious ● terrified ● wary ● worried ● annoyed ● aggravated ● dismayed ● disgruntled ● displeased ● exasperated ● frustrated ● impatient ● irritated ● irked ● angry ● enraged ● furious ● incensed ● indignant ● irate ● livid ● outraged ● resentful ● aversion ● animosity ● appalled ● contempt ● disgusted ● dislike ● hate ● horrified ● hostile ● repulsed ● confused ● ambivalent ● baffled ● bewildered ● dazed ● hesitant ● lost ● mystified ● perplexed ● puzzled ● torn ● disconnected ● alienated ● aloof ● apathetic ● bored ● cold ●

detached • distant • distracted • indifferent • numb • removed • uninterested • withdrawn • disquiet • agitated • alarmed • discombobulated • disconcerted • disturbed • perturbed • rattled • restless • shocked • started • surprised • troubled • turbulent • turmoil • uncomfortable • uneasy • unnerved • unsettled • upset • embarrassed • ashamed • chagrined flustered • guilty • mortified • self-conscious • fatigued • beat • burnt out • depleted exhausted • lethargic • listless • sleepy • tired • weary • worn out • pain • agony • anguished • bereaved • tense • anxious • cranky • distressed • distraught • edgy • fidgety • frazzled • irritable • jittery • nervous • overwhelmed • restless • stressed out • vulnerable • fragile • guarded • helpless • insecure • leery • reserved

(c) 2005 by Center for Nonviolent Communication
Website: www.cnvc.org Email: cnvc@cnvc.org
Phone: +1.505-244-4041

Exercise 2: Discover Your Voice

Write some advice you would like to give to this person when you are feeling defensive. Use the following words to create up to 5 suggestive statements for this person [Should, Need to, Shouldn't, and Ought to]. For example, you might write, "S/he ought to keep her opinions to herself," or "S/he shouldn't tell me what to do with my life," or "S/he needs to get a job."

1

2

3

4

5

Exercise 3: Explore Your Unmet Needs

Review your advice from the list above and contemplate what need is not being met by exploring the implication of each of your original statements. For example, when reflecting on the statement, "s/he shouldn't tell me what to do with my life," you may find that you are upset because you need acceptance and support for your well-being. The statement, "S/he needs to get a job," might be pointing to your own need for security and your fear for their well-being.

The following list of needs, compiled by the center for nonviolent communication, is neither exhaustive nor definitive. It is meant as a starting place to support anyone who wishes to engage in a process of deepening self-discovery and to facilitate greater understanding and connection between people. Reread your suggestive statements from exercise two and circle the positive feelings, below, you would rather experience when interacting with this person.

- affection • appreciation • belonging • cooperation • communication • closeness • community • companionship • compassion • consideration • consistency • empathy • inclusion • intimacy • love • mutuality • nurturing • respect/self-respect • safety • security • stability • support • to know and be known • to see and be seen • to understand and be understood • trust • warmth • physical well-being • air • food • movement/exercise • rest/sleep • sexual expression • safety • shelter • touch • water • honesty • authenticity • integrity • presence • play • joy • humor • peace • beauty • communion • ease • equality • harmony • inspiration • order • autonomy • choice • freedom • independence • space •

spontaneity • meaning • awareness • celebration of life • challenge • clarity • competence • consciousness • contribution • creativity • discovery • efficacy • effectiveness • growth • hope • learning • mourning • participation • purpose • self-expression • stimulation • to matter • understanding

(c) 2005 by Center for Nonviolent Communication
Website: www.cnvc.org Email: cnvc@cnvc.org
Phone: +1.505-244-4041

CHAPTER 5
IDENTIFY ALOOF BEHAVIOR

Recognizable Behavior of an Aloof Response

- Passive verbal and nonverbal behavior

- Comes off detached and unaffected

- Tends to walk away

- Needs a lot of space or "me" time

- Resists being pinned down [contracts]

- Condescending and analytical [mostly in their own self talk]

- Difficulty making up their minds

- Likes privacy and low commitment

- Feels distant and unapproachable

Common Communication Pattern of Aloof Behavior

- "It doesn't matter; I don't care"

- "I am no threat; you can decide"

- An aloof sticks to conversations concerning their experiences/emotions

Power Moves used by Aloof Behavior to Elicit Attention from Others

- Appears mysterious to be drawn out

- Forces others to engage in an undeserved investment of energy to gain commitment, information and emotion, which is usually shared in a direct way by others

- When approached, they retract

Point of View/Potential Underlying Fear of Aloof Behavior

You may be wondering why some people engage in aloof behavior. Behavior is perpetuated by fear. For example, if you are afraid of a snake, you might jump up and run away when you come across one. Some common fears of people who engage in aloof behavior are that potentially anything they say or do will be held against them and others cannot be trusted with information.

These fears are intense and very real to the individual who holds them. They may have an underlying belief that mirrors, "most everything I share with others is used to hurt me." They feel the need to protect themselves and stay at a distance from others and when this doesn't happen they use aloof behavior to ensure it will.

Common Destructive Communication Strategies of Aloof Behavior

- Stonewalling - withdrawing from the interaction, appearing stiff, glancing away

- Indifference - "whatever works; you decide; it doesn't matter to me."

An Aloof Often Uses an Avoiding Conflict Response Style

During an intense interaction, the interpersonal style of conflict you will typically find coupled with aloof behavior is avoidance. Avoiding messages include feelings of, "Let's leave well enough alone" and "I'll think about it tomorrow" and like a turtle, avoiders are willing to withdraw from an interaction.

Common avoiding behavior includes the ability to reduce tension in a group, as they know how to successfully "buy time." They will allow others to do and go first. They focus on and manage issues of low importance within a group of people [family or workplace] and often find themselves in a low power position. They will demonstrate noncommittal behavior and deny a conflict when it is occurring; this is often done by changing the topic. They may subscribe to the idea that "snide remarks are fair."

Avoiders are skilled at many things. They have the ability to withdraw from an intense interaction with others and their sense of timing is impeccable and often quite stealth. They can sidestep an uncomfortable conversation topic and have the ability to simply walk away from a conflict. In other words, they are comfortable with leaving things unresolved.

There are a number of positive and negative consequences that result from avoiding behavior. If avoidance is overused it will result in the lack of input from others and major group decisions will be made by default. If the avoider does so for too long, interpersonal issues will start to fester and a cautious group climate will arise.

If avoiding behavior is underused and the avoider starts to come out of the shell that others are used to experiencing her/him in, s/he will find s/he now has too many causes to tackle and this will result in the lack of prioritization and delegation across the group members. Hostility and hurt feelings will likely manifest.

Most people who predominantly exhibit aloof behavior initially approach conflict with a response that suggests, "Let's think/talk about this later." However, when engaged in an intense interpersonal drama, which ends with the aloof feeling defeated, you can expect them to exhibit behavioral responses in this order during the escalation: aloof, poor me, interrogator and then they will end with intimidator behavior.

What You'll Experience in the Presence of Aloof Behavior

- A lack of disclosure about common information

- A threat of being left or abandoned

- Vagueness or unresponsive behavior

- A feeling that they are preoccupied

- A lack of concern or apathy

- Little to no interest in you

- A feeling that they are being secretive

- A feeling of "high maintenance," as you'll be forced to have to "work" for information

Why Am I Uneasy in the Presence of Aloof Behavior?

Aloof behavior will evoke particular feelings for the receiver as these responses control us around our common human need for validation and connection with others. In other words, aloof responses play off of our need for contact with others and self-confidence and this is how we both plug into and are controlled by them. The underlying feeling of an aloof response is "I am distant, vague and distracted so you should work on drawing me out." To maintain inner balance in the presence of aloof behavior we need to overcome our negative personal emotions related to these fears or we may give our power and energy to them and/or lose our acceptance and love for them. Below are some examples of common thoughts and feelings that arise in the presence of aloof behavior:

> - "I feel threatened and believe this person will leave me or abandon me completely."
>
> - "I feel unworthy as s/he shows little to no interest in me."
>
> - "I feeling s/he is not being honest with me, as s/he seems to have many secrets s/he won't share."
>
> - "I feel this person doesn't care for me, respect me or trust when s/he does not communicate."
>
> - "When s/he doesn't communicate with me, I feel like I have done something wrong."
>
> - "I need to communicate with him in order to solve problems and make decisions."
>
> - "I cannot be happy without communication with her/him."

- "I need his/her attention in order to feel I am interesting and have self-worth."

- "I feel rejected because s/he will not pay attention to me."

- "I feel all alone in the world as s/he has withdrawn from me and my needs."

- "I feel frustrated because it is both unfair and unjust to exclude me."

- "If s/he cared for me, then s/he would communicate with me."

- "I must lack self-dignity if this person is not paying attention to me."

- "I am being ignored as s/he does not openly share her/his feelings and thoughts."

- "I feel unloved when this person doesn't respond to me or give me any attention."

- "I feel angry because s/he is not giving me what I need in this interaction or relationship."

- "I am unworthy of love when s/he ignores me."

- "I feel lonely when s/he doesn't share or communicate with me."

- "I feel alienated with her/him because s/he doesn't open up to me."

- "I feel guilty and fear that I did something wrong to this person."

- "I am angry s/he thinks s/he can treat me this way."

- "I am drained of energy around this person and cannot offer anything in return to her/him."

- "I am frustrated and angry with her/him because s/he is preventing me from feeling good."

Aloof Behavior Elicits Negative Counter Behavior from Others

- An aloof will experience things they don't want, as decisions are made by default when opinions aren't openly expressed

- An aloof will often encounter issues and problems that fester

- An aloof will create a cautious climate where people withhold information as to not offend them

What Personal Benefits are Gained at the Expense of Using Aloof Behavior?

When someone engages in aloof behavior they will experience a number of personal benefits. Aloof behavior allows one to control others and essentially get their way with others by making people seek them out. The use of aloof behavior allows people to feel a false sense of security because when they are engaged in it:

> •They get to withdraw and gain self-worth as you try to draw them out and focus your attention on them.
>
> •They don't have to be burdened by helping others decide or express opinions or ideas because others have learned not to ask.
>
> •They aren't able to be hurt or controlled by others because as they distance themselves from honest emotional contact and often avoid meaningful interactions altogether.

Common Clashes to Aloof Behavior

An aloof tends to feel the most uncomfortable, misunderstood and defensive around people who tend to use intimidator behavior. There is an old adage that states, "what you don't like about others is usually something you don't like about yourself" and this saying starts to resonate upon further investigation as to why individuals with aloof and intimidator behavior do not intermingle well after long periods of time.

It has been previously noted that when an aloof is at his/her worst [defeated], s/he will go through the drama cycle and are forced to give in when they reach intimidator behavior. When an aloof spends time with people who use intimidator behavior, they are reminded of what they feel like and how they respond to others when they are at their worst and feeling weak. This can become downright repulsive when the intimidator behavior is recognized and fixated upon.

Common Alliances to Aloof Behavior

An aloof will often most strongly align with and defend family members and friends who tend to use aloof and poor me behavior. Simply put, an aloof understands, condones and can justify the behavior of another aloof and because of this, they often get along well. An aloof can abruptly extinguish poor me behavior with statements like, "uh huh, what," while they appear to not hear what the poor me is in the midst of saying, while, likewise, a poor me can abruptly extinguish aloof behavior with statements like, "what's wrong; I feel bad when you don't talk to me; did I do something to make you upset?"

When a control drama is called out and brought to the forefront, it cannot stay active for much longer and thus aloof and poor me behavior often cancel one another out. The result is that the two individuals will spend longer periods of time together. There also seems to be an unconscious understanding that if these two behavior types were to have a conflict, it could be intense because the aloof can withdraw and play the silent treatment for long periods of time and the poor me can hold a grudge/guilt for long periods of time. The risk is that the conflict might never end.

You will find that when two individuals have the same dominant control drama, yet they do not get along, it is usually based on one's rationale of the other's intention behind the behavior they are displaying. [i.e. It is said that "If you can spot it, you got it," meaning, the individual will clearly recognize the behavior, but doesn't agree with the other's use of it or the intended purpose behind it].

Common Long Term Attraction to Aloof Behavior

An Aloof tends to be most strongly drawn to and attracted to people who tend to use interrogator behavior. Those who use aloof behaviors like to be drawn out and interrogators have the stamina to continue to ask the questions needed to get the aloof's attention. Those who use interrogator behavior like to ask questions and focus the conversation around their interests and the aloof is comfortable listening for longer periods of time because they get to avoid disclosure.

Effective Approaches that Help Distance You from Aloof Behavior

- Ask directly about their reluctance to respond to you

- Avoid defensive behaviors, as it will fuel their anxiety and fear around mistrusting and they will further withdraw

- Name their game by specifically describing their behavior; they will either admit to the observations or withdraw from the relationship for a period of time

Maintain Inner Balance When Dealing with Aloof Behavior

When dealing with aloof responses, we need to deal with some personal emotions in order to stay steady in their presence and not be affected by them. You can use positive affirmations, like the examples below, to maintain balance when dealing with aloof behavior.

▪"Life gives me exactly what I need at every moment so that I can learn my next lesson in my growth process."

▪"I am not responsible for the other's silence."

▪"S/he can still love me and care for me even if s/he cannot readily express it."

- "Her/his aloofness is a result of her/his own fears and anxieties."

- "Giving her/him his freedom and space is the best way to allow her/him to open up."

- "S/he is not my only source of happiness in life."

- "My self-worth is not dependent on her/his ability to open up to me or not."

- "I can be fulfilled within myself even without someone to engage in conversation."

- "I can fulfill my needs by communicating with god daily."

- "I have many good friends and family members with whom I can communicate."

- "Be loving, allowing his freedom and accepting him as he is the best ways to encourage his opening."

- "Life gives me experiences I need so I can grow."

- "We all have different ways of viewing things."

- "I am not responsible for this person's choices."

- "People can get along and love each other even when they don't agree."

- "No one can use me so I will choose to give or not to give to this person."

- "I don't need to explain my decisions to this person."

- "This person is helping me better understand my own needs."

Understanding Aloof Behavior Leads to Acceptance and Forgiveness

How do you feel when you believe someone is intentionally withholding or withdrawing from you? Choose one specific person to focus on and be precise about what you think of that individual. I suggest you write down your feelings to really grasp how you experience this person and feel in their presence. How might you view that person differently once you can fully grasp and trust that "they do not know what they do?"

Most aloof behavior comes with the intention of ensuring their safety and trust with you and your life experience. Reexamine an intense interaction you've had with aloof behavior and see if you can change your point of view to now hear their message with the intention of protecting their feelings/ideas/privacy. How do you feel about this person when you don't see them as aloof? Is there any reason to keep labeling them this way? Move towards accepting the individual for who s/he is, knowing that "people don't change; responses change" and choose to change your responses when in the presence of aloof behavior. You are in control of your experiences with others and can choose whether or not you will engage their control drama.

Exercise 1: Work Through Your Personal Emotions Related to Aloof Behavior

Start by imagining someone who creates defensiveness within you through their aloof behavior. The following are words we use when we want to express a combination of emotional states and physical sensations. This list, compiled by the center for nonviolent communication, is neither exhaustive nor definitive. It is meant as a starting place to support anyone who wishes to engage in a process of deepening self-discovery and to facilitate greater understanding and connection between people. Circle the negative feelings that arise in you when you are interacting with this person:

- afraid ● apprehensive ● dread ● foreboding ● frightened ● mistrustful ● panicked ● petrified ● scared ● suspicious ● terrified ● wary ● worried ● annoyed ● aggravated ● dismayed ● disgruntled ●

displeased • exasperated • frustrated • impatient • irritated • irked • angry • enraged • furious • incensed • indignant • irate • livid • outraged • resentful • aversion • animosity • appalled • contempt • disgusted • dislike • hate • horrified • hostile • repulsed • confused • ambivalent • baffled • bewildered • dazed • hesitant • lost • mystified • perplexed • puzzled • torn • disconnected • alienated • aloof • apathetic • bored • cold • detached • distant • distracted • indifferent • numb • removed • uninterested • withdrawn • disquiet • agitated • alarmed • discombobulated • disconcerted • disturbed • perturbed • rattled • restless • shocked • started • surprised • troubled • turbulent • turmoil • uncomfortable • uneasy • unnerved • unsettled • upset • embarrassed • ashamed • chagrined flustered • guilty • mortified • self-conscious • fatigued • beat • burnt out • depleted exhausted • lethargic • listless • sleepy • tired • weary • worn out • pain • agony • anguished • bereaved • tense • anxious • cranky • distressed • distraught • edgy • fidgety • frazzled • irritable • jittery • nervous • overwhelmed • restless • stressed out • vulnerable • fragile • guarded • helpless • insecure • leery • reserved

(c) 2005 by Center for Nonviolent Communication
Website: www.cnvc.org Email: cnvc@cnvc.org
Phone: +1.505-244-4041

Exercise 2: Discover Your Voice

Write some advice you would like to give to this person when you are feeling defensive. Use the following words to create up to 5 suggestive statements for this person [Should, Need to, Shouldn't, and Ought to]. For example, you might write, "S/he ought to keep her opinions to herself," or "S/he shouldn't tell me what to do with my life," or "S/he needs to get a job."

1

2

3

4

5

Exercise 3: Explore Your Unmet Needs

Review your advice from the list above and contemplate what need is not being met by exploring the implication of each of your original statements. For example, when reflecting on the statement, "s/he shouldn't tell me what to do with my life," you may find that you are upset because you need acceptance and support for your well-being. The statement, "S/he needs to get a job," might be pointing to your own need for security and your fear for their well-being.

The following list of needs, compiled by the center for nonviolent communication, is neither exhaustive nor definitive. It is meant as a starting place to support anyone who wishes to engage in a process of deepening self-discovery and to facilitate greater understanding and connection between people. Reread your suggestive statements from exercise two and circle the positive feelings, below, you would rather experience when interacting with this person.

- affection • appreciation • belonging • cooperation
  • communication • closeness • community •
  companionship • compassion • consideration •

consistency • empathy • inclusion • intimacy • love • mutuality • nurturing • respect/self-respect • safety • security • stability • support • to know and be known • to see and be seen • to understand and be understood • trust • warmth • physical well-being • air • food • movement/exercise • rest/sleep • sexual expression • safety • shelter • touch • water • honesty • authenticity • integrity • presence • play • joy • humor • peace • beauty • communion • ease • equality • harmony • inspiration • order • autonomy • choice • freedom • independence • space • spontaneity • meaning • awareness • celebration of life • challenge • clarity • competence • consciousness • contribution • creativity • discovery • efficacy • effectiveness • growth • hope • learning • mourning • participation • purpose • self-expression • stimulation • to matter • understanding

(c) 2005 by Center for Nonviolent Communication
Website: www.cnvc.org Email: cnvc@cnvc.org
Phone: +1.505-244-4041

CHAPTER 6
IDENTIFY STRATEGIES TO BEST BALANCE A CONTROL DRAMA

STRATEGY #1

Control Dramas Affect Your Thoughts

When we interact with others and find that we need to defend ourselves and explain our worth to them, we start to put our focus, and even our emotions, onto them. In other words, it allows us to keep the focus off of ourselves and this means we do not have to look at ourselves in a real way. Control dramas often show up in our own thinking as we relive dialogue and scenes we've had with others. This is where we get caught up in the drama on the intrapersonal level of self-talk.

When we are caught up thinking about other peoples' problems and how they affect us, it leaves us with no one left to take care of ourselves. Are other people really that powerful over us? Who controls our thinking? Can we actually violate our own rights thinking about others' problems and tending to their issues over our own issues? Who could possibly be more significant to you than you? Of course we are all human and it is normal to reflect on the interactions we've had with others. What we may not realize is the individuals who throw us off balance are great gifts in our lives. They help us project our thoughts about ourselves and point us in the direction where we can best help ourselves.

Review Your Thoughts

On a deeper level we can take our self-talk and turn it inward to learn more about ourselves. Consider this for example, when you think someone is trying to be right and control you, don't you kind of want to be right and control them/the interaction? When you think someone is being rude and offending you, don't you kind of want to be rude back and offend them? Our personal thoughts and emotions are indicators to much deeper things. Can you see the correlation between what you accuse others of, and how that very thing starts to also arise in you? For example if you check your voicemail and hear your dad say, "I am not sure where you are right now but I would appreciate a call back -- preferably tonight;" your next thought might be, "my dad is so controlling." When you think your dad is so controlling you probably won't call him back right away because then he is "controlling you." So, you "control" him instead and decide to call him back another day.

Below write the names of five people you'd like to better understand. After each name, write down some familiar feelings or complaints that come to mind when you experience them:

1

2

3

4

5

Reframe Your Thoughts

If we are unable to find a problem with someone else's behavior, then we are likely comfortable with that behavior in ourselves. In other words, can you see how thoughts like, "s/he should respect me more" can turn into, "I should respect me more" or, "s/he should give me what I need" can translate into, "I should give me what I need." Can you see how thoughts such as, "s/he shouldn't tell me what to do" can translate into, "I shouldn't let her/him tell me what to do." When we can interact with others and find that they no longer irritate us to the level they once did, then we will know that we have begun to respect ourselves as we should and deserve to be respected.

Take time to review what you wrote and reflect on any underlying meaning or messages you discover from your words. Can you reframe what you wrote to fit you rather than the person to whom it was directed? How does it feel when you stop focusing on others and their behavior and turn inward to look at your own feelings and behavior? The answers may, indeed, be within.

STRATEGY #2

The Language within a Control Drama Lacks Accountability

When defensiveness is present in a conversation, it is likely your control drama will start to emerge. People feel the most defensive when messages of evaluation, control, hidden agendas, superiority, guilt, certainty and lack of emotion are present. In other words, these messages cause us to feel anxious or threatened; we don't trust the people around us; we receive messages that we are being evaluated; we receive hints to change your behavior; the messages we receive tend to have a hidden agenda, which is often coupled with guilt; the person/people we interact with act superior; there is a feeling of receiving messages of "certainty" when the speaker is delivering his/her ideas or opinions.

If you listen carefully to a conversation in the midst of defensiveness, where control dramas have surfaced, you will notice you can often hear and feel excuses being made. Excuses are often disguised and will, more than likely, come in the form of detailed explanations, emotions, denials, accusations, example giving and defensive nonverbal behavior [eye rolling, dramatic sighing]. Of course we all find ourselves engaged in this kind of communication during delicate moments and it is quite normal to choose to respond this way when we are feeling defensive. However, these forms of "excuse making," keep the issue/problem unresolved, active and "on the table." In other words, an Excuse = Blaming. When you don't take ownership for an issue, whether you are right or wrong, then the issue and the control drama remain active.

Communicating with Accountability Stops an Active Control Drama

Assertive communication contains a tone of accountability and puts the issue/problem in the "past." In other words Accountability = Ownership. Ownership stops the blame game and stifles control dramas. It is noteworthy to mention here that control dramas are also present in mindless gossip about others. When we talk about other people, even when they are not present, we tend to allow defensiveness back into the conversation. If you pay close attention to gossip, you will hear messages that contain opinions, emotions, judgments and blame moving to the forefront of the conversation and this allows conflict to stay active or even worse, it adds fuel to the drama.

How to Communicate with an Accountable and Drama Free Message

Below are the components needed when constructing an accountable and drama free message. If these components are present in your message to another during a difficult conversation, the conversation will be more balanced and thus more effective. You will then be able to, more readily, put the issue in the "PAST."

P Be sure to include a <u>Polite</u> and <u>Professional</u> introduction and maintain this tone throughout the interaction.
"I hope this email finds you well. I have been thinking about you since our last interaction."

A Be willing to <u>Apologize</u> for anything in which you are responsible, verbally <u>Agree</u> with one or more of their talking points, and find a quality or behavior of theirs you can <u>Appreciate</u> and <u>Admire</u> it aloud.

"I have come to realize it was wrong of me to talk poorly about our work processes to anyone other than our team and I apologize for doing so. Please know I realize how much time you put into these projects and appreciate your hard work."

S Tell them how you intend to/plan to <u>Solve</u> the issue at hand or ask them directly what can be done to resolve it.

"Next time I will…"

"How would you like me to handle discrepancies with our work orders as we move forward?"

T <u>Thank</u> them for the opportunity to meet/communicate and <u>Target</u> a positive interpersonal message.

"Thank you for hearing me out; I am glad we discussed this issue because I enjoy working with you and want to ensure we are on the same page."

STRATEGY #3

Set Healthy Boundaries and Find an Assertive Tone that Works for You

•Respond with a *Factual* Tone - a factual response gives facts, feedback or information and makes clear your needs, wants, beliefs, opinions and/or feelings.
"As I see it, our work relationship is going quite well."
"I'd like you to be here by 9 o'clock."
"I feel very pleased with the way the situation has been resolved."
"I liked the comments you included in our family Christmas letter."

•Respond with an *Empathetic* Tone - an empathetic response shows sensitivity that can be used to preempt an aggressive person, flowed by an expression of your needs and wants.
"I can see the new schedule means extra work for you until we hire a new person. Please know that I'd still like you to keep on working with it to ensure good customer service."
"Although I can see you're very busy at the moment, I

need your assistance with something, will you please help me?"

- Respond with a *Divergent* Tone - a divergent response can establish whether there has been a misunderstanding between what was previously agreed upon and what is actually happening.

"As I recall, we agreed that raking the leaves was our top priority today. You seem to be giving more time to cleaning out the gutters. Can we please clarify which has top priority?"

"We said we would hold meetings weekly. They seem to be monthly. We need to establish them regularly – every two weeks or every week as agreed."

- Respond with an *Expressive* Tone - an expressive response allows you to expresses your negative feelings, letting other people know the adverse effect their behavior is having on you without becoming overemotional.

"When you're late back from lunch and the phones are busy. I feel annoyed you're not here to help. I'd like you to come back on time and take your turn on the phones."

"I feel frustrated when you ask my staff for answers.

I'd like you to check with me first and if I can provide answers, I'll direct you to the right person."

- Respond with a *Consequential* Tone – a consequential response can be used as a warning when other people have failed to act, letting them know the consequences for their action, if they do not change their behavior.

"I'm not going to let any of my staff work on this project with your people, unless you give them access to the same training that your team was given."

"This client's order is worth thousands of dollars. If we fail to respond to questions quickly and lose the account, it will have an adverse impact on the group."

- Respond with an *Approachable* Tone - an approachable response finds out the other person's views, needs, wants, or feelings and to make sure that there is no misunderstanding between you.

"What problems might that create?"

"What would you prefer to do?"

"I'd like to hear your views on this topic."

"What do you think about xyz?"

"What are the pros and cons on this issue from your point of view?"

STRATEGY #4

How Do I Integrate My Feelings and Needs into Effective Communication with Others?

If you listen to others speak, you will often hear the phrase, "I feel…" Yet, when you hear them complete the sentence, there is no feeling associated with it. Someone might say, "I feel like you are lying" and this is not a feeling, it is an accusation that sets you up to be defensive. In other words, when we have a conversation with someone who steers us away from authentic feelings and mutual understanding, we often start a defensive communication pattern. In this cycle we will we create excuses for both ourselves and for others. For example we may blame ourselves and say, "Did I just interrupt you? I am seriously so annoying; I should just shut up already!" We might make excuses for others too and say, "If s/he would just shut up for a second, s/he would know that we need to be there by 5pm."

How does it feel when someone communicates without feelings? A non-defensive communication pattern creates responsibility and understanding for both ourselves and for others. We can do this by taking ownership of both our feelings and needs and say, "I am FEELING a bit embarrassed that I just interrupted you, I guess I NEEDED to make sure my question was answered; please know I won't do that again." We might create responsibility and understanding for others and say, "I wonder if s/he's FEELING rushed and NEEDS to be somewhere else soon and so s/he interrupted to ensure s/he understands the plan."

Redirect the Conversation Back to Feelings and Needs

Once you have found an assertive tone that works well for you, practice speaking to others based upon their human feelings and needs. Below are some examples:

Solve a Problem - "I'm sorry you feel tired, but you are still responsible for washing the dishes and I need to know this house is in order before we leave for the weekend."

Manage Behavior – "I am feeling overwhelmed because everyone seems to be talking at once and I need to know that you all hear what I am saying and understand our plan."

Respond to Another's Emotion – "So you are feeling frustrated about our relationship and need to know if you have done something to upset me?"

Offer Praise – "I noticed you worked three late shifts in a row. It made me feel secure in hiring you because you demonstrated understanding of our recent staffing needs."

Compromise – "I am feeling stuck on this issue and need to know you are committed to attending these meetings. Can you email me when you know you are going to be late or miss a meeting?"

Reflect on the language used in the previous statements above and work to create some feelings/need statements of your own using the suggestions below:

"I need _____ and feel _____. Can you _____?"
"Do you feel _____ because you need _____?"

"I feel _____ because I need _____. Are you willing to help me?"

"Your need for _____ must make you feel _____. How can I help you?"

"I am feeling _____ and need to _____."

STRATEGY #5

Being Present with Someone *is a* Response

When someone is responding in an ineffective way through an intense control drama, follow the steps below to defuse the situation.

1] Respond to them with flat and neutral statements that are concise [no more than 2 word responses – seriously]

"Thank You" – "Really" – "Oh" – "I See" – "Maybe"
"It Figures" - "Sure" - "That's Right" - "Of Course"
"Wow" – "Great" – "I Understand" – "Interesting"

2] Refrain from using any kind of a "MOVEMENT MESSAGE" [verbally or nonverbally]

Rolling eyes - Looking away - Walking away

Asking open ended questions – Withdrawing

3] Respond with a "STOP SIGNAL" [verbally or nonverbally]

Ask closed ended questions

Hold your palm up to them to indicate you'd like their behavior to "stop"

Remember "being present with someone is responding to them." You can sit in silence while offering them your intense presence and that alone will calm most people. Presence communicates an authentic message to the receiver such as, "I see you"; "I validate you" and "I understand and am listening to you," without you even having to say anything. Afterall, we are *human beings* and not *human doings*.

4]   State an objective [observable] fact and propose a solution

"You seem to be drinking a lot tonight; how about I take your son for a sleep over?"

"I noticed that you removed yourself from your assigned seat; how about we move you to the back table?"

"It appears as though you might become emotional; could we talk about this later?"

FINAL POINTS TO PONDER

People will continue to be who they are no matter what you think of them. You may not be able to change others, but you can work to better understand them. The more you understand someone, the easier it is to interact with them and forgive them. Most of us want to get along with others and like who we see, in the mirror, at the end of the day.

When you choose a conscious assertive response, it allows you to communicate in an authentic way and feel good about your communication with others. Keep in mind that "people don't change; responses change." Choose wisely and implement the inspirational words of Ram Dass, "turn your melodrama into mellow drama."

ABOUT THE AUTHOR

Dr. Jody Janati teaches in the Communication Studies Department at the University of Minnesota. She has an Ed.D. degree in Organizational Leadership and her primary interest area pertains to interpersonal conflict resolution strategies. As an author and independent consultant, she offers a variety of public and professional workshops on conflict reduction tactics and effective interpersonal communication skills. There are a number of conflict management workshops offered each year, yet rarely does the facilitator tell participants exactly what should be said or done when dealing with a difficult interaction. Dr. Janati focuses on a step by step approach.

"People don't change; responses change"
www.communicationinnovation.vpweb.com
651.210.2246 | norri125@umn.edu

Contact the author for additional copies of this book